EMOTIONOMICS

HOW FEELINGS DRIVE FINANCIAL CHOICES

Ramesh Chauhan

Dedication

To all those who seek a deeper understanding of the forces driving their financial decisions, and to those striving to achieve a balance of financial prosperity and emotional well-being. May this journey empower you to master your mind, your emotions, and ultimately, your financial future.

Epigraph

"Money has no life of its own; it is what we project onto it."
— Anonymous

Disclaimer

This book provides general information and is intended to promote a better understanding of the role emotions play in financial decisions. It is not intended as financial advice and should not be used as a substitute for the guidance of licensed financial professionals. Readers should consult with qualified advisors for financial planning and investment decisions that suit their individual needs.

Acknowledgements

I extend my heartfelt gratitude to everyone who has contributed to the creation of this book. Special thanks to my students and readers who, through their curiosity and questions, inspired the exploration of emotional influences on financial decisions. To my friends, family, and colleagues who provided unwavering support, encouragement, and feedback throughout this journey—thank you. Your guidance has enriched both this work and my understanding of the emotional complexities of personal finance.

Finally, I am grateful to those pioneering researchers, psychologists, and financial thinkers whose work has shaped my perspectives. It is my hope that this book, in turn, will contribute to a meaningful dialogue on the intersection of emotion and economics.

Preface

The journey of understanding money is often framed solely in terms of numbers, calculations, and cold hard logic. Yet, my decades of teaching and observing human behavior have shown me that emotions, rather than reason alone, frequently guide our financial choices. This book arose from my fascination with the unseen forces shaping our financial lives—emotions like fear, greed, envy, and the powerful sway of social pressures.

Through *Emotionomics*, I invite you to explore these hidden drivers, to question the impulses that steer your choices, and to discover new strategies for achieving a fulfilling financial life. My hope is that this book will not only broaden your understanding but also empower you to make financial choices that reflect both your aspirations and inner values.

Prologue

Imagine the rush of excitement as you watch a stock soar, or the pang of regret after a splurge you can't quite justify. Our financial choices, often portrayed as products of pure calculation, are steeped in emotion. But what if, by understanding these emotions, we could transform our financial behaviors from impulsive to intentional?

This book is about unraveling that mystery—about uncovering the emotional influences that shape our financial choices and showing how, by recognizing and managing these feelings, we can attain a more balanced and rewarding relationship with money.

CONTENT

- Dedication 3
- Epigraph 3
- Disclaimer 3
- Acknowledgements 4
- Preface 5
- Prologue 6

Introduction: The Emotional Economy of Money 10

    Exploring the Emotional Side of Financial Decisions 10

    A Story of Financial Impulse 11

    The Journey Ahead 12

Part 1: The Emotional Triggers Behind Financial Choices ... 15

    Chapter 1: Fear—The Power of Loss Aversion 17

        Why Fear Dominates Financial Decisions 17

        Understanding and Managing Financial Fear 18

        Moving Forward Without Fear 21

    Chapter 2: Greed—The Pull of "More" and the Risks of Overreach 22

        The Allure of Accumulation 22

        Finding Satisfaction and Setting Limits 23

        Embracing "Enough" 25

        Moving Beyond Greed 26

    Chapter 3: Envy—Financial Comparisons and the Desire to Keep Up 28

- The High Cost of Comparison 28
- Creating Your Own Financial Path 29
- Embracing Your Unique Financial Journey 32

Chapter 4: FOMO—Fear of Missing Out on the Next Big Opportunity 34
- The Urge to Join Financial Fads 34
- Practicing Financial Patience 35
- Embracing Patience in the Age of FOMO 38

Part 2: Emotions and Everyday Financial Choices ... 39

Chapter 5: Spending—When Emotions Drive Purchases 41
- The Emotional Drivers Behind Spending 41
- Mindful Spending Practices 42
- Building a Healthier Relationship with Spending 45

Chapter 6: Saving—Overcoming Emotional Hurdles to Build Wealth 47
- The Challenge of Delayed Gratification 47
- Building a Consistent Saving Habit 48
- Building a Wealth Mindset Through Consistent Saving 51

Chapter 7: Investing—Staying Calm in a Volatile Market 53
- Navigating Emotions in Investment Decisions .. 53
- Sticking to a Strategic Investment Plan 54
- Investing with Emotional Intelligence 57

Chapter 8: Debt—Facing the Emotional Weight of Borrowing 59
    The Emotional Toll of Debt 59
    Developing a Healthy Approach to Debt 60
    Taking Back Control 63

Part 3: Breaking Free from Emotional Financial Traps 65
    Chapter 9: Recognizing Your Financial Triggers 67
    Chapter 10: Building Emotional Resilience for Financial Stability 72
    Chapter 11: Reframing Financial Challenges as Opportunities 77
    Chapter 12: Strengthening Emotional Intelligence in Financial Choices 82

Part 4: Building a Balanced, Fulfilling Relationship with Money 89
    Chapter 13: Rethinking Wealth Beyond Monetary Success 91
    Chapter 14: Practicing Gratitude and Contentment in Financial Life 96
    Chapter 15: Making Intentional Financial Choices Through Mindfulness 102

Conclusion: The Path to Emotional Mastery in Financial Decisions 109

Introduction: The Emotional Economy of Money

Exploring the Emotional Side of Financial Decisions

When it comes to managing money, we often think of it as a numbers game. There are spreadsheets to track, budgets to balance, and savings plans to strategize. Financial advice tends to be centered around rational choices: how to save, where to invest, what not to buy. Yet, for many of us, these calculations are only part of the story. Beneath the surface, our financial decisions are influenced by something far less predictable and far more powerful—our emotions.

Emotions like fear, greed, envy, and even joy play a massive role in our relationship with money. These emotions, often simmering below the surface, can make us impulsive or hesitant, reckless or overly cautious. We might tell ourselves that buying that new gadget or luxury handbag is a rational choice, but more often than not, there's an emotional driver at play—a desire for status, a need for comfort, or a momentary thrill. Understanding these emotional undercurrents is critical, because while they can drive us to make choices that feel good in the moment, they often lead to regret in the long term.

In this book, we'll dive deep into this "emotional economy" of money, examining how our feelings shape our financial decisions in ways we're often not even aware of. By understanding and managing these emotions, we can make smarter, more intentional financial choices that align with our long-term goals.

Emotionomics :How Feelings Drive Financial Choices

A Story of Financial Impulse

Let me share a story that might feel familiar. Meet Sarah. A few years ago, Sarah was at a stable place in her career, earning a good salary and feeling confident about her future. She'd saved a bit, but like many people, she couldn't resist checking her investment app during her lunch breaks. She'd been reading about a new tech stock that was "guaranteed to skyrocket." Everyone was talking about it, from her coworkers to her friends on social media.

In the excitement of the moment, Sarah decided to invest a significant portion of her savings in this stock. She felt a thrill, a surge of optimism. After all, she didn't want to miss out on the opportunity that everyone else seemed to be jumping on. But as weeks turned into months, the stock began to plummet. The excitement quickly turned into panic, then regret. Sarah was left with a fraction of her original investment and a painful lesson about emotional decision-making.

Sarah's story is not unique. Every day, people make impulsive financial decisions driven by emotions, whether it's buying into a stock market frenzy, splurging on luxury items they don't need, or avoiding critical financial decisions out of fear. These choices often leave us feeling disillusioned and frustrated, wondering why we acted so irrationally. The truth is, financial decisions are rarely as logical as we'd like to believe. Emotions are constantly at play, influencing us in subtle but powerful ways.

Sarah's experience underscores a simple but profound truth: mastering our financial lives requires more than just understanding budgets, interest rates, or investment portfolios. It requires understanding ourselves.

The Journey Ahead

So, what can we do about it? How can we stop our emotions from derailing our financial lives? This book is here to answer those questions.

In the chapters that follow, we'll explore the hidden emotional drivers behind our financial behaviors. We'll look at why fear holds us back from taking risks that could benefit us, and why greed can push us into risks that are reckless. We'll delve into how envy and social comparisons lead us to spend beyond our means, and why the need for security sometimes drives us to hoard rather than invest wisely. Each chapter will uncover a different aspect of the emotional economy of money, showing you how these emotions shape your financial choices in ways you may not even realize.

But this book is not just about understanding these emotions. It's about learning to manage them, to harness them in ways that support rather than sabotage your financial goals. You'll find real-life stories, psychological insights, and practical strategies designed to help you recognize and navigate your financial emotions. By the end, you'll have a toolkit for making decisions that are not only financially sound but also emotionally wise.

In essence, this book is an invitation to take control of your financial life by first taking control of your emotional life. Financial freedom isn't just about numbers on a spreadsheet—it's about having a healthy, balanced relationship with money, one that isn't ruled by fleeting feelings or external pressures.

As you turn the pages, I encourage you to keep an open mind and to approach your financial habits with curiosity and honesty. The journey to financial well-being is not just about learning new skills—it's about unlearning old habits and beliefs that no longer serve you.

Welcome to *Emotionomics: How Feelings Drive Financial Choices*. Let's embark on this journey together to understand the emotional side of money and, ultimately, to empower you to make choices that bring not just financial success, but peace, balance, and fulfillment.

Part 1: The Emotional Triggers Behind Financial Choices

Chapter 1: Fear—The Power of Loss Aversion

Why Fear Dominates Financial Decisions

Fear is one of the most primal and powerful emotions we experience, and it has a profound influence on our financial choices. At the heart of this fear lies a psychological concept known as **loss aversion**—a tendency to prefer avoiding losses over acquiring equivalent gains. This means that the pain of losing $100, for example, is often felt more acutely than the joy of gaining $100. While this instinct to avoid loss was helpful for survival in ancient times, in today's financial landscape, it can lead to overly cautious decisions that prevent us from taking advantage of growth opportunities.

Consider this: you're given a choice between a guaranteed $1,000 or a 50% chance of winning $2,000 (and a 50% chance of getting nothing). Many people would instinctively choose the guaranteed $1,000, even though the second option has the potential for a higher reward. This is fear of loss at work. The thought of possibly losing out on money can feel so unsettling that we tend to gravitate toward safer, but often less rewarding, choices.

This fear-based approach can be particularly detrimental in the world of investing. For instance, people who are overly afraid of market fluctuations may avoid investing altogether, sticking solely to savings accounts or low-yield bonds. While these choices may feel "safe," they can hinder long-term financial growth. When we prioritize avoiding loss over potential gains, we limit our opportunities and, in many cases, settle for outcomes that may not serve our future goals.

Fear, then, is a double-edged sword in financial decision-making. While some level of caution is beneficial—especially when it prevents reckless choices—an excessive focus on avoiding losses can ultimately lead to missed opportunities and diminished returns. Understanding and managing this fear is essential for making balanced and growth-oriented financial decisions.

Understanding and Managing Financial Fear

If fear is such a powerful and pervasive force in our financial lives, how do we keep it in check? The key lies in adopting strategies that allow us to recognize and manage our fear, rather than letting it dictate our decisions. Here are some practical steps to help you navigate financial fear with confidence and clarity:

1. **Define Your Financial Goals**
   One of the main reasons fear takes over is because we lack a clear sense of direction. When our goals are vague, every fluctuation in the market or potential loss feels like a threat to our financial stability. Start by defining specific, long-term financial goals—whether that's saving for retirement, building a college fund, or accumulating wealth for future opportunities. Clear goals give you a roadmap, which can help reduce anxiety when faced with short-term setbacks.
2. **Adopt a Long-Term Mindset**
   Financial markets fluctuate. That's a given. But people who get caught up in the day-to-day ups and

downs often make impulsive decisions based on fear rather than strategy. By adopting a long-term mindset, you can learn to ride out short-term volatility without panic. Understand that most investments, particularly in the stock market, need time to grow. Focus on the big picture rather than obsessing over every dip in value.

3. **Diversify Your Investments**

   One of the best ways to manage fear in investing is through diversification. By spreading your investments across different asset classes (stocks, bonds, real estate, etc.), you reduce the impact of a poor performance in any single area. This approach can help you sleep better at night, knowing that all your eggs aren't in one basket. Diversification mitigates risk, which in turn can ease the fear of loss and allow you to approach investing with a more balanced mindset.

4. **Educate Yourself About Risk**

   Many people fear financial decisions because they don't fully understand the risks involved. Fear often arises from uncertainty and lack of knowledge. The more you learn about investing and financial planning, the more empowered you'll feel. Take the time to understand how different types of investments work, and consult with financial professionals if needed. Knowledge is a powerful antidote to fear.

5. **Practice Mindfulness and Emotional Awareness**

   Mindfulness techniques, such as deep breathing or journaling, can help you become more aware of your emotional responses to financial situations. When you notice yourself feeling fearful, take a moment to pause and reflect rather than reacting impulsively. Ask yourself, "Is this fear based on an actual threat, or is it my mind's way of trying to protect me from an uncertain future?" Sometimes, simply acknowledging your emotions can help reduce their power over you.

6. **Reframe Your Perspective on Loss**
Rather than viewing every loss as a failure, consider it a learning opportunity. Losses are an inevitable part of financial growth, and every investor, no matter how successful, has experienced setbacks. The goal is not to avoid loss entirely but to learn from it and make better choices moving forward. When you start seeing losses as valuable feedback rather than threats, you'll be less afraid to take calculated risks.

7. **Focus on What You Can Control**
Fear often arises from focusing on things beyond our control, such as market fluctuations or economic conditions. While you can't control the stock market, you can control your savings rate, your spending habits, and how diversified your investments are. By focusing on these controllable factors, you can channel your energy into actions that move you closer to your goals, rather than being paralyzed by fear of the unknown.

8. **Set Up a Financial Safety Net**
Having an emergency fund can significantly reduce financial anxiety. When you know you have a cushion to fall back on, you're more likely to take calculated risks without being overwhelmed by fear. Aim to save at least three to six months' worth of living expenses in a readily accessible account. This safety net provides peace of mind and can

help you feel more secure in making investment decisions.

Moving Forward Without Fear

Fear will always be part of the financial journey, but it doesn't have to control it. By understanding the nature of fear and implementing strategies to manage it, you can move forward with greater confidence. You can shift from a mindset of fear-driven scarcity to one of growth-oriented abundance. Remember, the goal is not to eliminate fear but to make decisions that are informed, balanced, and aligned with your long-term objectives.

In this chapter, we explored the role of fear and loss aversion in financial decisions, but it's just one piece of the puzzle. As we move forward, we'll continue to uncover other powerful emotional triggers—like greed, envy, and the need for social validation—that shape our financial lives. Each of these emotions has its own set of challenges and solutions, and understanding how they work is the key to taking control of your financial future.

Let's continue the journey into the emotional world of finance, one emotion at a time, as we work toward a healthier, more empowered relationship with money.

Chapter 2: Greed—The Pull of "More" and the Risks of Overreach

The Allure of Accumulation

Greed is a powerful force that fuels the desire for "more." It's a deeply ingrained part of human nature, rooted in survival instincts that have driven us to accumulate resources for safety and security. However, in modern financial life, this drive for more can often spiral into something harmful—leading to risky decisions, excessive spending, and the constant pursuit of unsustainable growth.

Consider the countless examples of people jumping into speculative markets, hoping for massive returns in a short period. Think of the cryptocurrency booms, the housing bubbles, or the tech stocks that seem unstoppable—until they're not. The allure of "more" can be intoxicating, pulling even the most cautious investors into situations where they're risking more than they can afford to lose.

Why do we chase "more"? Part of it is psychological. The thrill of accumulation and the promise of future gains activate the brain's reward system, releasing dopamine—the same neurotransmitter responsible for feelings of pleasure and reward. It's why a rising stock portfolio or a new luxury purchase can feel so satisfying, at least temporarily. Greed, then, is not just about money; it's about the emotional high that comes with each incremental gain, each new asset, each notch of perceived success.

But while this hunger for more can fuel ambition and drive, it often leads to what psychologists call the "hedonic treadmill"—the never-ending pursuit of bigger goals, more money, more stuff, without ever reaching a point of lasting satisfaction. It's like climbing a mountain where the peak always seems just out of reach. You achieve one financial milestone, but instead of feeling content, you immediately set your sights on the next.

The danger here is that greed can cloud judgment and push people toward impulsive or overly aggressive financial decisions. They might pour money into speculative investments, chasing quick returns without considering the risks, or they may overspend on lifestyle upgrades, believing that more luxury will lead to more happiness. Ultimately, this constant push for "more" can lead to significant financial stress and the very real possibility of loss.

Finding Satisfaction and Setting Limits

If unchecked, greed can become a cycle that leads to burnout, financial strain, and even personal dissatisfaction. But there is a way to break this cycle and build a healthier relationship with money. The key lies in cultivating satisfaction with what we have, setting clear boundaries on our financial goals, and practicing gratitude for the present.

1. **Set Realistic Financial Goals**
   One of the most effective ways to counter greed is by setting specific, achievable financial goals. Instead of aiming for "more," define what "enough" looks like for you. For example, rather than simply wanting to "get rich," you could set a goal to save a certain amount for retirement, create an emergency fund, or reach a target income level that allows for a

comfortable lifestyle. When you have clear goals, it's easier to avoid the endless chase for more and focus on achieving meaningful milestones that align with your values.

2. **Practice Gratitude**

   Greed often stems from a mindset of scarcity—the fear that what we have will never be enough. Practicing gratitude can help shift this mindset by focusing on what's already good and fulfilling in your life. Consider keeping a gratitude journal where you write down things you're thankful for, both financial and non-financial. By recognizing the value of what you already have, you can reduce the impulse to constantly seek more and find satisfaction in the present.

3. **Limit Exposure to Triggers**

   Just as marketers are adept at creating desire, our surroundings can constantly trigger our greed. Advertisements, social media, and even well-meaning friends can influence us to want more. To counter this, limit your exposure to environments that fuel comparison or desire. For instance, if seeing luxury lifestyles on social media makes you feel inadequate, consider reducing your screen time or unfollowing accounts that don't contribute positively to your mindset. Awareness of these triggers can help you make more intentional choices rather than succumbing to external pressures.

4. **Avoid the Temptation of "Hot Tips" and Quick Wins**

   Financial greed often manifests in the form of jumping into "hot" investments or speculative ventures promising quick returns. Avoid the temptation to chase these high-risk opportunities.

Remember that true wealth-building is a marathon, not a sprint. When you find yourself tempted by a high-stakes investment, pause and ask yourself whether it aligns with your long-term financial plan or if it's simply an emotional response to the desire for quick gains.

5. **Build a Balanced Financial Portfolio**
A diversified, balanced portfolio helps protect against the emotional pull of greed. When your investments are spread across different asset classes and risk levels, you're less likely to feel compelled to chase high-risk, high-reward options. This approach not only stabilizes your financial foundation but also reduces the chances of significant losses. Balanced financial planning allows you to enjoy steady growth without needing to pursue "the next big thing."

6. **Reflect on the Real Meaning of Wealth**
What does wealth mean to you? Take time to define what a wealthy life looks like beyond just financial measures. For many, true wealth includes quality time with loved ones, good health, personal growth, and the freedom to pursue passions. When you broaden your definition of wealth, you're less likely to measure your success solely by financial accumulation and more likely to find fulfillment in diverse aspects of life.

Embracing "Enough"

At the core of managing greed is learning to appreciate "enough." The modern world constantly pushes us to want more—more money, more possessions, more success. But the pursuit of more, without a clear purpose, often leaves us feeling unfulfilled. Embracing "enough" doesn't mean giving up on ambition; it means finding satisfaction in the journey rather than fixating on an elusive destination.

The art of wealth-building lies not just in the accumulation of assets but in knowing when to pause, appreciate, and recalibrate. True financial wisdom isn't about endlessly increasing your net worth—it's about understanding what brings you peace, joy, and fulfillment. By recognizing when enough is enough, you can avoid the risks and stress that come with unchecked greed and instead build a life of balanced wealth.

Moving Beyond Greed

Greed is an emotion that, when managed well, can fuel ambition and drive. But when left unchecked, it becomes a trap, leading to financial overreach, dissatisfaction, and even failure. To build sustainable wealth, you must learn to balance ambition with contentment, and goals with gratitude.

As we continue this journey through the emotional drivers of financial decisions, remember that money is only a tool. The real measure of wealth lies not in how much you accumulate, but in how you use it to live a life that aligns with your values and brings you genuine fulfillment.

In the next chapter, we'll examine another powerful emotion that influences financial behavior: envy. Unlike greed, which is often about wanting more for oneself, envy arises when we compare our financial status to others. Just like greed, it can lead to irrational decisions if left unchecked, and understanding its impact is key to achieving financial peace.

Chapter 3: Envy—Financial Comparisons and the Desire to Keep Up

The High Cost of Comparison

Envy is a powerful emotion—one that, in the financial world, often manifests as the urge to "keep up with the Joneses." Social comparison is deeply embedded in human nature; we measure ourselves against others as a way to understand our own place in society. In the past, this might have meant comparing homes, clothes, or cars with neighbors and colleagues. But in today's world, social media has amplified this instinct, exposing us to the curated lifestyles of countless people around the globe.

Consider this: you're scrolling through Instagram and see a friend from college vacationing in the Maldives, a high school classmate buying a new luxury car, or a coworker posting about their newly renovated home. These glimpses of others' financial achievements—or at least, what they choose to showcase—can easily trigger feelings of inadequacy. This can lead to financial decisions driven not by personal goals or values, but by a desire to "keep up" with what others seem to have.

Social media often serves as a kind of highlight reel, where people show only their best moments, creating an illusion of perpetual success and luxury. In reality, these snippets rarely reveal the whole picture. We don't see the credit card debt, the sleepless nights, or the sacrifices made to afford those luxury items. Yet, without these details, it's easy to fall into the trap of comparison, assuming others are more successful or happier because of their material possessions.

This cycle of comparison can lead to a range of negative financial behaviors:

- **Overspending** on luxury items or vacations simply to feel equal or superior to others.
- **Taking on unnecessary debt** to fund a lifestyle that aligns with societal expectations rather than personal needs.
- **Investing impulsively** in risky assets or trends because "everyone else" seems to be doing it, leading to financial decisions that lack careful planning.

Envy, when unchecked, can push us away from our financial goals and priorities. It creates a sense of urgency to "catch up" or "prove ourselves," often at the expense of financial stability. But the truth is, constantly comparing our financial progress to others' is not only unhealthy but also unsustainable. The people who appear to "have it all" are likely dealing with their own financial stressors, insecurities, or compromises.

Creating Your Own Financial Path

Breaking free from the cycle of comparison and envy isn't easy, especially in a world where we're constantly bombarded with images of other people's successes. However, by focusing on our own financial goals, we can reclaim control over our decisions and align our spending with what truly matters to us.

Here are some strategies for shifting the focus from others' financial lives to your own:

1. **Define Your Financial Values and Goals**
   The first step in resisting the pull of comparison is to establish your own financial values and goals. What does financial success look like for you? It may not mean owning a luxury car, buying an expensive home, or traveling to exotic destinations. Financial goals that reflect your values might include achieving debt-free status, building an emergency fund, funding your children's education, or investing in experiences that bring you joy. When you have a clear understanding of your own priorities, it becomes easier to recognize when you're being influenced by external pressures. Try creating a "financial vision board" or writing down your top three financial goals as a daily reminder to stay focused on what truly matters to you.

2. **Limit Exposure to Social Media and Consumer Triggers**
   Social media and advertising are designed to create desire and envy. If you find that certain apps or accounts make you feel inadequate or trigger impulsive spending, it may be beneficial to limit your exposure. Consider curating your social media feeds to include content that aligns with your values or inspires you in positive ways, rather than making you feel pressured to spend. You can also set time limits on certain apps or schedule "social media detoxes" to remind yourself that there's more to life than what's shown on a screen. Remember, your self-worth is not measured by your financial status or material possessions.

3. **Practice Gratitude and Contentment**
One of the most effective ways to combat envy is to cultivate gratitude for what you already have. Practicing gratitude shifts the focus from what you lack to what you already possess, reducing the desire for more. Consider keeping a gratitude journal where you note down the things you're thankful for each day, both big and small. Contentment doesn't mean you lack ambition or stop striving for improvement; rather, it's about recognizing that your happiness and worth are not dependent on external validation. By focusing on the present and appreciating what you have, you can build a foundation of inner peace that isn't easily shaken by others' achievements.

4. **Create a Spending Plan That Reflects Your Values**
A spending plan, or values-based budget, can help you stay true to your financial goals and reduce the influence of envy on your decisions. When you allocate your resources based on your values, you're more likely to feel satisfied with your choices and less compelled to spend on things that don't align with your priorities. For example, if travel and personal growth are important to you, allocate a portion of your budget toward those areas instead of luxury items that don't resonate with your core values. Knowing that you're spending intentionally on things that genuinely matter to you can reduce the urge to "keep up" with others.

5. **Remind Yourself of the Hidden Costs**
It's easy to envy someone's apparent financial success without considering the potential hidden

costs. Remind yourself that people often make significant sacrifices to afford a certain lifestyle—whether it's taking on debt, working long hours, or experiencing high levels of stress. Recognize that the appearance of wealth doesn't always equate to financial health or personal happiness. Reflect on the costs that come with constantly chasing a lifestyle that's out of alignment with your values. By prioritizing financial health over appearances, you're investing in a future that is stable and fulfilling rather than fleeting and costly.

6. **Focus on Long-Term Fulfillment Over Short-Term Status**

   Short-term decisions often lead to regret, especially when they're driven by envy. Instead of trying to keep up with others for the sake of appearances, focus on decisions that will bring you long-term satisfaction and stability. Ask yourself, "Will this make me happier in the long run?" This question can help you make choices that align with your true desires rather than transient feelings of envy.

Embracing Your Unique Financial Journey

Everyone's financial journey is different. What works for one person may not work for another, and that's okay. The key to lasting financial satisfaction is embracing your unique path, focusing on your values, and ignoring the noise of comparison. Envy can be a powerful driver, but it doesn't have to dictate your financial choices.

By creating a life centered around your own financial goals and values, you'll find that the need to "keep up" with others fades. Instead, you'll be free to pursue a path that's meaningful to you, building a sense of contentment that no amount of comparison can undermine.

In the next chapter, we'll dive into another powerful emotion that impacts financial behavior: guilt. While envy pushes us to acquire and consume, guilt often leads us to self-sabotage, causing feelings of regret or shame in our spending and saving habits. Understanding guilt's influence is essential for creating a balanced and healthy relationship with money.

Chapter 4: FOMO—Fear of Missing Out on the Next Big Opportunity

The Urge to Join Financial Fads

In today's hyper-connected world, where news and social media constantly bombard us with the latest "can't-miss" opportunities, it's no surprise that FOMO—or the *Fear of Missing Out*—has become a powerful force in our financial lives. FOMO can make even the most rational people feel as though they're missing out on something big if they don't jump on a particular investment, purchase, or trend immediately. The problem? This fear often leads to impulsive, poorly thought-out financial decisions that don't align with long-term goals.

We've seen FOMO manifest in a variety of financial contexts. Think of the cryptocurrency boom when people across the world rushed to invest in Bitcoin, Ethereum, and other digital assets, driven by stories of everyday people turning modest investments into small fortunes. Many jumped in without fully understanding the complexities or risks, simply because they didn't want to be left behind. The same can be said for stock market fads, real estate bubbles, and even the frenzied rush to buy "must-have" consumer products.

FOMO is particularly insidious because it taps into a very primal human instinct: the fear of exclusion. We worry that by not participating, we might lose out on a life-changing opportunity or fall behind our peers. It doesn't help that social media amplifies this feeling by showcasing success stories, often without context. For example, you might see someone post about their gains from a recent investment, but they rarely mention the losses they endured along the way or the sleepless nights they spent worrying about market crashes.

Consider the story of a young investor named Sam, who, in the midst of the cryptocurrency surge, put his entire savings into a popular digital coin. He had been skeptical at first, but after seeing friends and influencers bragging about their gains, he couldn't resist. Sam feared that if he didn't act fast, he'd miss out on a once-in-a-lifetime chance to grow his wealth. However, soon after he invested, the market crashed. Sam was left with significant losses and a hard lesson: the rush to seize "opportunities" often overlooks the risks involved.

FOMO doesn't just impact investments; it influences all kinds of financial decisions, from real estate purchases to joining high-cost networking programs or seminars that promise "exclusive insights." The result is often the same: people spend money they can't afford to lose, driven by a fear of missing out rather than careful, considered planning.

Practicing Financial Patience

So, how do we combat FOMO? The key lies in cultivating financial patience and developing a clear, long-term perspective. Here are some strategies to help ground your financial decisions in intentionality rather than impulse:

1. **Recognize and Question Your Motivations**
   When you feel the urge to jump into a financial trend, pause and ask yourself why. Are you genuinely interested in the investment or product, or

are you just reacting to a sense of urgency and hype? Sometimes, just recognizing that FOMO is at play can be enough to take a step back and reassess. A helpful question to ask is, "Would I still make this decision if no one else knew about it?"

2. **Define Your Financial Goals**
Having clear financial goals can serve as an anchor in times of uncertainty. When you know what you're working toward—whether it's retirement, buying a home, or building an emergency fund—it becomes easier to filter out distractions and avoid investments or purchases that don't align with your objectives. Ask yourself: "Does this decision help me move closer to my financial goals, or is it simply a reaction to external pressure?"

3. **Educate Yourself Before Acting**
Many FOMO-driven decisions happen because people don't fully understand what they're getting into. Take the time to research before making any major financial decision. With investments, for example, get to know the basics of how markets work, understand the risks, and consider your own risk tolerance. The more informed you are, the less likely you'll feel pressured into a decision by hype or speculation.

4. **Set Up a "Cooling-Off" Period**
If you're about to make a big financial move, try implementing a 24-hour or even week-long cooling-off period. Use this time to reflect on your decision. Often, the initial rush of excitement or fear of missing out will subside, allowing you to approach the decision more calmly and rationally. If, after the cooling-off period, you still feel strongly about the opportunity, you can proceed with more confidence.

5. **Limit Exposure to Hype-Driven Media**
Social media and news outlets often feed into FOMO by sensationalizing financial trends or success stories. Limit your exposure to these sources, or curate your feed to focus on reliable, balanced financial information rather than hype. Instead of following influencers or accounts that flaunt quick gains, seek out sources that provide long-term, stable financial advice.
6. **Practice Gratitude for What You Have**
FOMO is often fueled by a sense of lack—of not having enough. Practicing gratitude can counter this feeling by helping you appreciate what you already have. When you focus on the financial security and assets you've already built, you're less likely to feel compelled to chase after every "next big thing."
7. **Reframe Your Understanding of Opportunity**
Remember that financial opportunities come and go, and no single trend or investment is going to make or break your financial future. FOMO often makes us believe that if we miss out on something now, we'll never get another chance. But opportunities are abundant. Focus on finding opportunities that fit your strategy and risk tolerance, rather than scrambling to join every new wave.
8. **Evaluate Long-Term Value Over Short-Term Gains**
FOMO often leads us to chase quick wins at the expense of long-term stability. Instead of focusing on potential short-term gains, assess whether an opportunity will hold value over time. Will it contribute to your financial well-being in the years to come, or is it a fleeting trend? Sustainable wealth-

building requires patience and a focus on enduring value.

Embracing Patience in the Age of FOMO

Patience is a rare but essential virtue in personal finance, especially in today's world, where everything seems immediate and everyone appears to be achieving success overnight. Embracing patience can give you a powerful edge, helping you make decisions based on your own goals and values rather than reacting to external pressures.

By cultivating patience, you're not just building a strong financial foundation; you're also building emotional resilience. You learn to trust in your own path, recognizing that the journey to financial success is personal and doesn't require you to keep up with others.

In the next chapter, we'll explore another emotional trigger that often leads to financial mistakes: guilt. While FOMO pushes us to spend impulsively, guilt can cause us to self-sabotage or make overly conservative decisions that hold us back. By understanding the role of guilt, we can create a healthier, more balanced relationship with our finances.

Part 2: Emotions and Everyday Financial Choices

Chapter 5: Spending—When Emotions Drive Purchases

The Emotional Drivers Behind Spending

Money is more than a tool for transactions; it's also a vehicle for expressing and managing emotions. For many of us, spending isn't just about fulfilling practical needs—it's often an emotional experience that can be driven by excitement, anxiety, boredom, or even sadness. Think about the times you've indulged in "retail therapy" after a rough day or made an impulsive purchase just because it felt good in the moment. Emotional spending, while often satisfying in the short term, can lead to long-term regret, debt, and even shame as we try to balance our financial well-being with our emotional needs.

Consider Sarah, a successful young professional who frequently finds herself shopping online late at night. After a long, stressful day at work, browsing her favorite stores becomes a form of relaxation and escape. She adds items to her cart, feeling a rush of excitement as she imagines wearing that new outfit or using the latest gadget. However, when the packages arrive a few days later, the thrill has faded, leaving her with items she doesn't really need and a growing credit card bill that triggers feelings of guilt and stress.

This pattern is common. Many people use spending as a way to cope with stress, boredom, or low self-esteem, only to realize that it doesn't bring lasting happiness. Emotional spending can become a cycle: we buy to feel good, regret it, and then buy again to cope with that regret. Over time, this pattern can lead to significant financial strain, as well as a feeling of being trapped in an endless cycle of consumption without true satisfaction.

Emotional spending can take many forms, such as:

- **Impulse Buying:** Making spontaneous purchases without considering long-term consequences. Often, these decisions are driven by the desire for an immediate reward or escape from an uncomfortable emotion.
- **Retail Therapy:** Shopping as a form of emotional comfort, often used to manage stress, loneliness, or sadness.
- **Keeping Up with Appearances:** Spending to impress others or fit in with a certain social circle, often motivated by feelings of inadequacy or a desire for validation.

While spending can provide a temporary sense of relief, it rarely addresses the underlying emotional needs. Instead, it often leads to regret, financial anxiety, and even shame. The key to breaking this cycle lies in understanding our emotional triggers and adopting strategies that allow us to spend mindfully and intentionally.

Mindful Spending Practices

The first step in managing emotional spending is awareness. By recognizing the feelings that drive our spending habits, we can start to regain control over our finances and make choices that truly align with our values and goals. Here are some practical techniques for cultivating mindful spending:

1. **Create a "Cooling-Off" Period** One of the most effective ways to curb impulsive spending is by implementing a cooling-off period. When you feel the urge to make a non-essential purchase, wait at least 24 hours before completing the transaction. For larger purchases, extend the waiting period to a week or even a month. This gives you time to assess whether the item is something you truly need or simply an emotional impulse. During this time, ask yourself questions like, "Will I still want this a week from now?" and "How does this purchase fit into my long-term financial goals?" Often, the initial excitement fades, and you realize the item isn't as essential as it seemed in the heat of the moment.
2. **Identify Your Spending Triggers** Emotional spending often stems from specific triggers. These might include stress from work, feelings of loneliness, or even certain environments, like browsing shopping apps on your phone at night. Spend some time reflecting on when and why you tend to spend impulsively. Do you shop more when you're bored? When you've had a bad day? Identifying these triggers can help you anticipate and manage emotional spending before it starts. Once you know your triggers, consider alternative ways to address these emotions. For example, if you shop when you're stressed, try exercising, meditating, or talking to a friend instead. If boredom leads to browsing online stores, replace that habit with an engaging hobby or activity that brings you satisfaction without spending.
3. **Set Intentional Spending Goals** Having clear, intentional spending goals can help you make more

mindful decisions. Start by defining what truly matters to you—whether it's saving for a vacation, building an emergency fund, or simply enjoying occasional, guilt-free treats. When you have specific goals, it's easier to evaluate whether a purchase aligns with those priorities. For instance, if you're working toward a debt-free life, ask yourself, "Does this purchase bring me closer to my financial goals?" Setting boundaries around spending categories—such as a monthly budget for dining out or entertainment—can also help you manage expenses without feeling deprived.

4. **Practice Gratitude to Combat the Urge to Spend**
Often, the impulse to spend comes from a sense of lack—the feeling that we don't have enough or aren't enough. Practicing gratitude can help shift your focus from what you don't have to what you already possess. By regularly reflecting on the things you're grateful for, you may find that the desire to accumulate more stuff diminishes. Try keeping a gratitude journal where you list three things you're thankful for each day. This simple exercise can reduce the feeling of scarcity that drives many emotional purchases, fostering contentment and helping you appreciate the value of what you already own.

5. **Plan for Emotional Spending in Your Budget**
Recognize that it's unrealistic to eliminate emotional spending entirely. Instead, plan for it. Create a small budget specifically for "fun" or discretionary spending. This allows you to indulge occasionally without guilt, while still keeping your overall financial plan on track.

Knowing you have a set amount for occasional treats or spontaneous purchases can help you resist impulsive buys outside that budget. You're less likely to feel deprived, and more likely to enjoy the purchases you make, knowing they're part of a balanced financial plan.

6. **Use Cash for Discretionary Purchases** Studies show that we tend to spend less when we use cash instead of credit cards. The physical act of handing over cash makes us more conscious of the money we're spending. For discretionary purchases, consider using cash instead of cards. It's a simple way to make spending feel more "real," helping you think twice before buying.

7. **Reflect on Your Purchase Afterward** After making a purchase, take a few moments to reflect on how you feel. Did the item bring you the satisfaction you expected? Are there any regrets? By examining your emotions post-purchase, you can gain insights into your spending patterns and make adjustments moving forward. This reflection can help you distinguish between purchases that genuinely enhance your life and those that only provide a temporary boost.

Building a Healthier Relationship with Spending

Spending money is an inevitable part of life, and there's nothing wrong with enjoying your purchases. However, when spending becomes a way to cope with emotions, it can lead to financial instability and emotional distress. By understanding the emotional drivers behind spending, you can begin to make more intentional choices, using your money in ways that bring genuine value and joy to your life.

Mindful spending isn't about depriving yourself—it's about aligning your financial behaviors with your deeper values. When you shift your focus from impulsive purchases to intentional spending, you'll likely find that you feel more satisfied and empowered in your relationship with money.

In the next chapter, we'll dive deeper into the psychology of financial security, exploring why so many of us struggle to save and how our emotional needs for safety and control play into our savings habits.

Chapter 6: Saving—Overcoming Emotional Hurdles to Build Wealth

The Challenge of Delayed Gratification

Saving money might seem straightforward on paper—simply set aside a portion of your income and let it grow over time. However, in practice, saving consistently can be incredibly challenging. The difficulty lies in the psychology of delayed gratification and the natural human preference for immediate rewards over distant benefits. This tendency, known as **present bias**, often leads us to favor spending now rather than saving for the future.

Imagine you've just received a paycheck. You know that putting some of it into a savings account would be the "responsible" choice, yet the allure of spending on things that bring immediate pleasure—dining out, new clothes, or the latest tech gadget—can be hard to resist. After all, the future feels abstract, while the joy of a purchase is right here, right now. This is the dilemma that people face every day: balancing today's desires with tomorrow's security.

There's a reason saving can feel like an uphill battle. Evolutionarily speaking, our brains are wired for short-term survival rather than long-term planning. In our ancestors' world, prioritizing immediate needs was essential; hoarding resources for the future often didn't make sense in uncertain, precarious conditions. However, in today's world of modern finance, this same survival instinct can sabotage our financial goals.

For example, consider the difference between spending $100 today on a nice dinner versus saving it for your retirement, which may be decades away. While saving that $100 could contribute to future financial security, it doesn't offer the instant pleasure of a delicious meal or an exciting experience. Overcoming this emotional barrier requires more than just willpower—it demands a shift in mindset and the development of strategies that make saving feel as rewarding as spending.

Building a Consistent Saving Habit

Understanding the emotional hurdles to saving is the first step, but the real challenge is finding ways to overcome these barriers and build a sustainable habit. Here are some practical strategies for developing a consistent saving habit, even when instant gratification pulls you in the opposite direction:

1. **Automate Your Savings**
One of the simplest ways to save consistently is to remove the decision from your hands entirely. By automating your savings, you create a system where a portion of your income is transferred to your savings account as soon as you're paid, before you even see it. This strategy leverages the principle of "out of sight, out of mind," making it easier to save because you don't experience the temptation to spend that money. Consider setting up automatic transfers to a separate savings account—perhaps even one that's less accessible, like an online bank with no debit card. Automation helps you make saving a default action, so even if you're tempted to spend, the money is already moving toward your goals without any additional effort on your part.

2. **Set Achievable Short-Term Goals**

   One of the reasons saving can feel daunting is because we often set goals that are too big or too distant. Saving for retirement or a house down payment can seem like a far-off dream, which makes it hard to stay motivated. To counter this, break down your savings goals into smaller, short-term milestones that feel more attainable and rewarding.

   For instance, if you're aiming to save $10,000 over the next two years, set a goal of saving $400 each month instead. Every time you hit one of these smaller goals, celebrate your progress. This can help create a sense of accomplishment and keep you motivated over the long term. Small wins build momentum, making the process feel less overwhelming and more satisfying.

3. **Visualize the Future Benefits**

   One powerful way to overcome present bias is to make the future feel more tangible. Research shows that visualizing your future self and future goals can increase your willingness to save. When you can picture the benefits of saving—whether it's financial freedom, a comfortable retirement, or the ability to travel—you're more likely to prioritize it over immediate spending.

   Try this exercise: Spend a few minutes each day visualizing the life you want to build through saving. Imagine yourself achieving that goal, whether it's living debt-free, owning a home, or enjoying retirement without financial worries. Picture the security, peace of mind, and satisfaction that come with it. By connecting emotionally with your future, you can make saving feel as rewarding as spending.

4. **Reward Yourself Along the Way**
Saving doesn't have to feel like deprivation. One way to keep it sustainable is by creating small, guilt-free rewards along the way. This might mean allowing yourself a treat every time you reach a certain savings milestone, such as $500 or $1,000. The reward doesn't have to be extravagant—it could be a nice dinner, a small gadget you've been eyeing, or a fun experience. The goal is to create a balance between saving and enjoying life in the present. By integrating rewards, you give yourself something to look forward to, which can make the act of saving feel like a positive experience rather than a sacrifice.

5. **Create a "Fun Fund" for Impulsive Spending**
While saving is essential, it's also unrealistic to expect that you'll never have moments of spontaneous spending. Instead of trying to eliminate impulse buys entirely, create a "fun fund" that allows for occasional indulgences. Set aside a small amount each month specifically for discretionary spending, whether it's on dining out, shopping, or entertainment. By setting boundaries around impulsive purchases, you prevent them from derailing your larger financial goals. The fun fund gives you permission to enjoy yourself without guilt, while your main savings goals stay protected. This balance between structured saving and planned indulgence can help you avoid burnout and make the saving process more enjoyable.

6. **Use Visual Tools to Track Progress**
Visual aids like charts, graphs, or even a simple savings tracker can make a big difference in your motivation. Watching your progress over time, even if it's slow, can be incredibly satisfying. For instance, you could create a chart that shows how much you've saved each month toward a particular goal. Each time you make a deposit, fill in a section of the chart and watch your progress grow. Seeing your savings add up provides a sense of accomplishment and reminds you that every small contribution counts. Over time, these visuals can become a powerful motivator, reinforcing the habit and making it easier to continue building your wealth.

7. **Reframe Saving as Self-Care**
Shift your perspective on saving by seeing it as an act of self-care. Just as you might invest in physical health through exercise or mental well-being through meditation, saving is an investment in your future financial health. Instead of viewing saving as a restriction, think of it as an essential practice for your long-term security and peace of mind. When you view saving as a way to take care of yourself, it becomes a positive choice rather than a burden. Every dollar saved is a step toward financial independence, security, and the ability to handle future challenges with confidence. Reframing saving in this way can make the practice feel more empowering and rewarding.

Building a Wealth Mindset Through Consistent Saving

Saving money isn't just about the financial benefits—it's also about building a wealth mindset. When you commit to a consistent saving habit, you develop discipline, patience, and the ability to delay gratification. These qualities are essential not only for financial success but also for personal growth.

Remember, saving is a journey, and it's okay to start small. Each deposit, no matter how modest, brings you closer to your financial goals. By overcoming the emotional hurdles and integrating mindful saving practices into your life, you can build a strong foundation for wealth and well-being.

In the next chapter, we'll explore how to transition from saving to investing—a step that many find intimidating due to the risk involved. We'll look at the psychology behind risk aversion and discuss strategies for building confidence in making investment decisions.

Chapter 7: Investing—Staying Calm in a Volatile Market

Navigating Emotions in Investment Decisions

Investing is often touted as the best way to build wealth over time, but it comes with a significant emotional challenge: staying calm when the market gets turbulent. As much as investing involves financial knowledge and strategic planning, it also requires emotional resilience. This chapter dives into the psychological side of investing, exploring how our emotions—especially fear and overconfidence—can lead us to make irrational, and often costly, financial decisions.

Imagine you've invested in the stock market, and suddenly, there's a market downturn. It's all over the news; experts are predicting another recession, and you watch your investments lose value day by day. The fear of losing your hard-earned money kicks in, making you anxious and tempted to sell off your assets before they lose more value. However, reacting out of fear often leads to poor timing, as many people sell low and miss out on the eventual recovery.

On the other hand, think about a booming market where everyone is making money. Perhaps you feel an urge to invest more, confident that this upward trend will continue indefinitely. Overconfidence leads many investors to make impulsive, high-risk investments, hoping for quick profits. But markets are unpredictable, and this kind of reactive decision-making often results in losses when the bubble bursts.

Both fear and overconfidence are powerful emotions that can derail even the most thoughtful investment strategy. The key to long-term success in investing is to manage these emotions and avoid making decisions based solely on market fluctuations. Instead, cultivating a calm, steady approach can help you make sound investment choices, regardless of market conditions.

Sticking to a Strategic Investment Plan

The foundation of successful investing lies in having a clear, strategic plan. This plan should be based on your long-term financial goals, risk tolerance, and time horizon. A well-thought-out investment plan can serve as your anchor during periods of market volatility, helping you stay focused and avoid making impulsive moves.

Here are some practical strategies to help you stick to your plan and manage your emotions in the ups and downs of the market:

1. **Define Your Investment Goals and Risk Tolerance**
   Before diving into any investment, it's crucial to define what you're trying to achieve. Are you investing for retirement, a child's education, or perhaps a down payment on a house? Having specific goals provides a sense of purpose, which helps you stay focused during market fluctuations. Additionally, understand your risk tolerance—how much risk you're comfortable taking. If you have a low risk tolerance, you may prefer a more conservative portfolio with bonds and blue-chip stocks, whereas someone with a higher risk

tolerance might lean toward growth stocks or other high-risk assets.

2. **Diversify to Reduce Risk**
One of the most effective ways to manage risk—and by extension, your emotions—is through diversification. By spreading your investments across various asset classes (stocks, bonds, real estate, etc.), industries, and geographic regions, you reduce the impact of a downturn in any single area. When your portfolio is diversified, you're less likely to experience drastic losses, which helps you stay calm during volatile markets. Diversification can give you the confidence that even if one investment underperforms, others will help balance it out.

3. **Automate Your Investments**
Automating your investments is a powerful way to remove emotions from the equation. Set up a system where a portion of your income automatically goes into your investment accounts, whether it's through a retirement plan like a 401(k) or automatic transfers to a brokerage account. This practice, known as dollar-cost averaging, allows you to invest consistently over time, buying more shares when prices are low and fewer when prices are high. Automation prevents you from overthinking or trying to time the market, both of which can lead to emotional decisions.

4. **Focus on the Long Term**
Market volatility is inevitable. Prices go up, and they go down—sometimes dramatically. But if you look at historical data, you'll notice that markets generally trend upward over the long term. By adopting a long-term perspective, you can avoid

getting caught up in short-term fluctuations that cause anxiety and lead to reactive decision-making. Remind yourself that investing is a marathon, not a sprint, and that short-term losses don't necessarily indicate a long-term problem.

5. **Practice Mindfulness and Emotional Awareness**
When market volatility makes you anxious, practicing mindfulness can help you manage your emotions. Take a step back and recognize how you're feeling. Are you fearful? Impatient? Greedy? By acknowledging these emotions, you're less likely to act on them impulsively. Simple mindfulness techniques, like taking a few deep breaths or stepping away from the screen, can help you stay grounded and make rational decisions. Recognize that emotions are a natural part of the investing experience, and allow yourself to feel them without letting them dictate your actions.

6. **Tune Out the Noise**
The financial media thrives on creating urgency, often amplifying market movements and encouraging reactive behavior. While it's good to stay informed, overconsumption of financial news can lead to anxiety and the feeling that you need to constantly adjust your investments. Avoid this trap by limiting your exposure to financial news, especially during turbulent times. Instead, set aside specific times to review your investments and financial goals—quarterly or annually is often sufficient for most people. This way, you're making adjustments based on your personal plan rather than reacting to market noise.

7. **Have a "Rules-Based" Investment Approach**
Consider creating a set of personal investment rules

to guide your actions. For instance, you might decide that you won't sell any investments after a market decline unless your financial situation has fundamentally changed. Or, you could set a rule to rebalance your portfolio annually, regardless of market conditions. Having a rules-based approach can keep you disciplined and prevent you from making impulsive decisions driven by fear or greed. When emotions run high, these rules serve as a rational guide to keep you on track.

8. **Review and Adjust, But Don't Overreact**
While sticking to a plan is crucial, it's also important to periodically review your strategy to ensure it aligns with your changing goals and circumstances. Life changes—whether it's a new job, a growing family, or approaching retirement—may require adjustments to your investment plan. However, remember that reviewing and adjusting your portfolio doesn't mean reacting to every market movement. Make changes based on your life situation and goals, not on temporary market conditions.

Investing with Emotional Intelligence

Investing isn't just about money—it's about understanding yourself. Emotions will always play a role in financial decisions, but by recognizing and managing them, you can build a resilient approach to investing. Emotional intelligence in investing means being aware of your triggers, creating systems to support your goals, and learning to stay calm amidst market chaos.

The journey of investing is filled with highs and lows, but maintaining a steady course through volatility is what ultimately leads to success. By staying grounded, sticking to a plan, and embracing a long-term perspective, you can navigate the emotional challenges of investing and build a portfolio that aligns with your goals.

As we continue on this journey, the next chapter will explore an area of finance that impacts us all, often in subtle ways: spending. We'll dive into the emotional side of spending and discuss how to make purchases that truly bring satisfaction, rather than regret. Let's move beyond the world of investments to examine the daily financial decisions that shape our lives.

Chapter 8: Debt—Facing the Emotional Weight of Borrowing

The Emotional Toll of Debt

Debt isn't just a financial burden; it's an emotional one. Many people experience complex and often conflicting emotions around debt, ranging from shame and guilt to temporary relief or even denial. These feelings can weigh heavily on an individual's mental well-being, often leading to stress, anxiety, and even depression. Debt becomes more than just a number on a statement—it's a constant reminder of financial choices, and sometimes, financial mistakes.

Let's think about it this way: when someone takes on debt, it's often for something that feels necessary or desirable in the moment, whether it's paying for college, buying a car, covering medical expenses, or simply using a credit card to maintain a certain lifestyle. The initial decision may bring relief or satisfaction. However, as the bills start arriving and balances grow, these positive emotions are often replaced by negative ones. People might feel trapped, constantly reminded of past choices and the impact they have on their present.

One common emotional experience is **shame**—the feeling that debt signifies a personal failure or inability to manage money. Shame can lead people to hide their debt from family and friends, which in turn increases their isolation and anxiety. Another common feeling is **guilt**, especially when debt arises from overspending or impulse buying. Many people feel they've "failed" in some way, or that they're being irresponsible. Unfortunately, this guilt can make it harder to face the reality of the debt, leading some to avoid looking at their statements or actively planning for repayment.

Debt can also lead to **fear**—fear of the future, fear of more debt, and fear of financial instability. Many people with significant debt worry about the implications of their debt on their lives: "Will I ever get out of this? Will I be able to retire? What if I lose my job?" This fear can be paralyzing, making it difficult for people to take positive action toward reducing their debt. And then there's **denial**, where some people try to ignore their debt altogether, hoping it will somehow disappear. This can lead to a vicious cycle where avoidance only makes the problem worse.

Understanding the emotional impact of debt is essential because it's often these feelings that prevent people from tackling their debt head-on. The cycle of guilt, shame, and avoidance keeps people stuck, unable to make progress and feel empowered about their finances.

Developing a Healthy Approach to Debt

So, how can people face their debt without becoming overwhelmed by the emotional toll? The key is to develop a healthy and proactive approach to debt management, one that acknowledges the emotional weight but doesn't allow it to dictate behavior. Here are some practical strategies for managing debt effectively and emotionally.

1. **Acknowledge Your Emotions About Debt**
   The first step in managing debt is acknowledging the emotions that come with it. Ignoring or

suppressing these feelings won't make them disappear, and they can often grow stronger in silence. Take a moment to reflect on how debt makes you feel—whether it's shame, guilt, fear, or even anger. Simply acknowledging these emotions can help you feel more in control and reduce the power they have over you. Journaling or talking to a trusted friend or financial counselor about these feelings can be a helpful first step.

2. **Reframe Debt as a Temporary Challenge, Not a Life Sentence**

    Debt can feel overwhelming, especially when balances are high, but it's essential to remember that debt is not a permanent condition. By reframing debt as a temporary challenge, you can take a more optimistic and empowered approach. Rather than thinking, "I'll never get out of debt," try to focus on smaller, manageable steps you can take now. This mindset shift can reduce feelings of helplessness and help you approach debt as a solvable problem.

3. **Build a Realistic Repayment Plan**

    One of the most effective ways to tackle debt is to create a structured repayment plan. When you have a plan, you're not just reacting to the problem; you're taking control. List all of your debts, including interest rates and minimum payments, and prioritize which ones to pay off first. You might choose to focus on paying off high-interest debt (often called the avalanche method) or start with the smallest balances for quick wins (the snowball method). By breaking down the debt into smaller, manageable goals, you'll feel a sense of progress that can boost your motivation.

4. **Avoid Emotional Borrowing**

   Many people get into debt because they borrow for emotional reasons, such as stress relief or impulse spending. Becoming aware of these triggers is crucial. If you notice that you're tempted to borrow or spend during times of stress, anxiety, or sadness, take a pause and consider alternative coping mechanisms. For instance, instead of shopping as a way to relieve stress, try going for a walk, meditating, or calling a friend. Developing healthier coping strategies can help you avoid adding more debt in moments of emotional vulnerability.

5. **Practice Self-Compassion**

   Debt can lead to intense feelings of self-criticism, but beating yourself up won't make the debt go away. Instead, practice self-compassion by acknowledging that everyone makes financial mistakes, and you're not alone. Many people face debt at some point in their lives, and it's not a reflection of your worth or abilities. Treat yourself with kindness and understanding, and focus on taking small, positive steps rather than dwelling on past mistakes.

6. **Set Milestones and Celebrate Progress**

   Paying off debt is a marathon, not a sprint, so it's essential to recognize and celebrate your progress along the way. Set small milestones, such as paying off a particular balance or reducing your debt by a certain percentage, and reward yourself when you achieve them. These rewards don't have to be expensive; they can be simple treats or experiences that bring you joy. Celebrating progress helps maintain motivation and reminds you that you're moving closer to financial freedom.

7. **Seek Support**
Dealing with debt alone can be overwhelming, but there's no need to suffer in silence. Seek out support from trusted friends, family, or financial advisors who can offer guidance and encouragement. Many communities also have free or low-cost credit counseling services that can help you create a repayment plan and negotiate with creditors. Having someone to talk to about your financial struggles can reduce feelings of isolation and provide a source of accountability.

8. **Cultivate a Growth Mindset Toward Debt**
Instead of viewing debt as a failure, see it as an opportunity for growth and learning. A growth mindset allows you to look at debt as a chance to develop financial discipline, budgeting skills, and resilience. This perspective can make the process of repaying debt feel less like a punishment and more like a journey of self-improvement. Over time, the lessons you learn from managing debt can help you make smarter financial decisions in the future.

9. **Focus on Financial Education**
Sometimes, debt can feel overwhelming because of a lack of understanding. By improving your financial literacy, you'll feel more empowered to manage your money effectively. Educate yourself on topics like budgeting, interest rates, and credit scores. Knowledge is power, and the more you understand about your finances, the more confident you'll feel about managing and reducing debt.

Taking Back Control

Debt can feel like a heavy burden, but it doesn't have to control your life. By facing the emotional aspects of debt, building a structured repayment plan, and practicing self-compassion, you can work toward financial freedom in a way that feels empowering and manageable. Remember that every small step you take brings you closer to your goal.

Debt is a part of many people's lives, but it doesn't define your worth or your future. The journey to financial freedom is about resilience, growth, and learning to make choices that align with your long-term well-being. As we continue, let's shift our focus from the emotional weight of debt to the benefits of building healthy financial habits and embracing a balanced approach to money. In the next chapter, we'll explore the importance of cultivating a positive relationship with saving and investing for the future, setting the foundation for long-term wealth.

Part 3: Breaking Free from Emotional Financial Traps

Chapter 9: Recognizing Your Financial Triggers

Identifying Emotional Cues in Financial Choices
Recognizing and understanding our emotional triggers is a vital first step toward making sound, rational financial choices. Emotions often influence financial behaviors in ways we don't even realize, subtly pushing us toward impulsive spending, excessive saving, or hasty investments. By becoming aware of these emotions and their impact, we can begin to make choices that better serve our financial goals.

Certain emotional triggers are especially common in financial contexts. Here are three key examples:

- **Stress**: Financial stress can arise from many sources—debts, unexpected expenses, job insecurity, or economic downturns. When we're stressed, we're more likely to make reactionary decisions, such as liquidating investments during market dips or overspending on comfort items to feel an immediate sense of relief. These behaviors, however, often lead to more stress in the long term. Recognizing how stress affects your financial actions is critical to breaking the cycle.
- **Boredom**: Boredom may seem harmless, but it's a surprisingly powerful trigger, especially in our consumer-driven society. People may browse shopping sites or make spontaneous purchases simply out of a desire to pass the time or add excitement to their routine. This type of spending can quickly add up and derail savings goals.

- **Social Comparison**: Comparing ourselves to others—whether friends, family, or social media influencers—can trigger spending to match others' lifestyles. This is often subconscious but can lead to financial strain if we prioritize others' standards over our own goals. Recognizing this trigger can help shift focus from external pressures to personal priorities.

By understanding these common emotional cues, readers can start to identify how similar patterns may appear in their own financial lives. Awareness of these triggers helps lay the groundwork for developing healthier habits and reducing emotional reactions in financial decisions.

Exercises for Emotional Awareness

To build this awareness, here are some exercises that can help you uncover your personal financial triggers and develop self-awareness. The more you understand your emotions in the context of financial decisions, the better equipped you'll be to respond intentionally rather than reactively.

1. **Journaling to Track Emotional Responses**
   One effective way to identify your emotional triggers is through daily or weekly journaling focused specifically on financial decisions. Here's how to get started:
   - **Create a Finance Journal**: Dedicate a notebook or digital document to your financial thoughts, feelings, and choices. Record any significant spending decisions, investment actions, or financial reflections.

- **Reflect on Emotional Patterns**: Write down the emotions you felt before, during, and after each financial choice. Did you feel stressed, excited, or pressured? For instance, if you bought something you didn't need, note whether you felt impulsive, bored, or envious. Over time, patterns will start to emerge, helping you pinpoint specific triggers.
- **Set Aside Time for Review**: At the end of each week or month, review your journal entries. Look for recurring triggers or circumstances that lead to certain financial behaviors. This reflection helps you become more aware of how your emotions influence financial decisions.

2. **Mindful Spending Pause**

This exercise encourages you to pause and check in with yourself emotionally before making any non-essential purchase. Here's how it works:

- **Set a Time Frame**: If you're about to make a purchase that isn't a necessity, implement a "pause" period—whether it's 24 hours or a few days. This cooling-off period can give you time to assess the emotional impulse driving the purchase.
- **Ask Reflective Questions**: During the pause, ask yourself questions like, "Am I buying this because I genuinely need it, or because I feel bored or pressured?" or "Is this purchase in line with my financial goals?" This reflection can help distinguish between a genuine need and an emotional impulse.

- **Decide with Intention**: At the end of the pause, decide if the purchase aligns with your goals and values. Often, by simply giving yourself time and space, the impulse fades, and you're left with a clearer sense of what truly matters.

3. **Creating an Emotional Trigger Map**
This exercise involves mapping out emotional triggers in different areas of your financial life:
   - **Identify Key Financial Areas**: List areas where you tend to feel emotionally reactive, such as spending, saving, investing, or managing debt.
   - **Associate Triggers**: For each area, identify the emotional triggers that come up. For example, stress might be a trigger in your savings plan, while envy might arise in spending decisions. This map helps visually connect emotions to specific financial behaviors.
   - **Develop a Response Plan**: For each trigger, create a response strategy. For example, if stress is a trigger in saving, your plan might be to focus on setting smaller, achievable goals. If social comparison triggers overspending, a response plan could involve unfollowing accounts that encourage competitive spending.

4. **Practicing Visualization for Financial Clarity**
This exercise is about using visualization to help center your emotions and focus on long-term financial goals:
   - **Set Your Financial Vision**: Take time to imagine what financial well-being means to

you, including how it would feel to be debt-free, have an emergency fund, or achieve other financial goals.
- **Use Visualization as a Grounding Tool**: When facing a financial decision or emotional trigger, take a moment to visualize this future state. This practice can remind you of your larger goals and help ground impulsive emotional reactions.
- **Incorporate Visualization into Routine**: Make it a habit to visualize your financial goals daily, especially during stressful or tempting financial situations. This consistent reminder strengthens your long-term mindset and helps counteract emotional triggers.

Chapter 10: Building Emotional Resilience for Financial Stability

The Importance of Mental Strength in Money Matters
Emotional resilience is essential for maintaining financial stability, helping individuals weather financial highs and lows without succumbing to impulsive or reactionary decisions. The ability to remain steady during times of financial stress—whether due to a market downturn, an unexpected expense, or even a sudden windfall—enables better decision-making and fosters sustainable wealth-building.

When people lack resilience, they're more likely to react emotionally to financial changes. For instance, during a market downturn, fear can lead to panic selling, locking in losses that might have been avoided with patience. In contrast, overconfidence during economic booms can lead to risky investments or overspending, with little consideration of long-term impacts. Resilience allows individuals to view these fluctuations from a balanced perspective, helping them remain committed to their financial strategies instead of being swayed by temporary emotional states.

Building emotional resilience also contributes to long-term wealth accumulation by supporting a consistent, disciplined approach to finances. Rather than relying on quick wins or giving in to setbacks, resilient individuals stay focused on their goals, understanding that financial growth often requires time, patience, and adaptability. Emotional resilience, in this sense, becomes a valuable asset, one that strengthens a person's ability to face financial challenges and achieve lasting stability.

Practices for Emotional Fortitude

Developing emotional resilience takes time and intention, but there are effective strategies that anyone can implement to help build this mental strength. Here are some actionable steps to cultivate resilience and fortify emotional stability in financial decision-making:

1. **Stress Management Techniques**
   Financial stress is one of the most common challenges people face, so managing it effectively is essential for resilience. Here are some ways to handle stress in money matters:
   - **Mindful Breathing**: Simple breathing exercises can provide immediate stress relief. When you feel anxious about a financial decision, take a few minutes to practice deep breathing, focusing on slowing down your breath. This helps regulate your nervous system, making it easier to approach financial issues with a clear mind.
   - **Regular Physical Activity**: Physical exercise releases endorphins, which are natural stress reducers. Activities like walking, yoga, or even stretching can alleviate tension and clear mental clutter, creating a more stable foundation for financial decision-making.
   - **Financial Check-ins**: Regularly reviewing your finances—whether weekly, monthly, or quarterly—can prevent stress from

accumulating. Check-ins help you stay aware of your financial position, making it easier to identify issues early and feel more in control.

2. **Practicing Mindfulness to Ground Financial Decisions**

Mindfulness is a powerful tool for developing resilience because it encourages a present-focused awareness, reducing the impact of impulsive emotional responses. Here are a few ways to integrate mindfulness into financial decision-making:

- **Mindful Decision-Making**: When faced with a financial choice, pause to examine your emotions before acting. Ask yourself questions like, "Am I feeling pressure to buy this because of stress, boredom, or excitement?" This reflective pause helps identify emotions that might be driving your decisions, enabling you to make a more intentional choice.
- **Regular Mindfulness Practices**: Try setting aside five to ten minutes a day for mindfulness meditation or reflection. Even a brief, daily practice can build resilience over time by increasing awareness of how emotions influence your thoughts, helping you detach from immediate impulses.
- **Financial Reflection Exercises**: Incorporate reflection questions at the end of each week to evaluate any financial decisions you made. Ask yourself, "Did I make decisions that were aligned with my goals? How did I feel while making these

choices?" This process helps reinforce mindful awareness and makes it easier to identify areas for improvement.

3. **Detaching from Immediate Emotional Impulses**
   One of the keys to resilience is learning to detach from emotions that drive immediate, often reactive choices. This doesn't mean ignoring emotions but rather creating a "mental space" between feeling and acting. Here's how to start detaching from financial impulses:
   - **Set Boundaries with Emotional Triggers**: If you know that certain activities—such as browsing online shopping sites or frequently checking the stock market—trigger impulsive financial behavior, create boundaries. For example, limit browsing time or establish specific times for reviewing investments.
   - **Use the "Wait and Reflect" Method**: Before acting on any significant financial decision, implement a 24-hour waiting period. This gives you time to evaluate the choice with a clear mind, reducing the impact of impulsive emotions. After the wait, ask yourself if the decision still feels aligned with your financial goals.
   - **Visualize Long-Term Goals**: When you feel the urge to make a spontaneous decision, take a few moments to visualize your long-term financial aspirations. This can help redirect focus from short-term satisfaction to long-term stability, making it easier to resist immediate impulses.

4. **Developing Positive Financial Habits**
   Consistent, small actions can build resilience by

reinforcing positive financial behaviors that buffer against emotional reactions. Here are a few habits to consider:

- **Create and Follow a Financial Plan**: Having a clear plan for saving, investing, and spending reduces uncertainty and helps guide decisions during times of stress or emotional highs. A well-structured plan can serve as an anchor, keeping you grounded in your long-term vision.
- **Celebrate Small Wins**: Recognize small accomplishments on your financial journey, whether it's sticking to a budget, avoiding an impulse purchase, or reaching a savings goal. Celebrating progress helps maintain motivation and builds confidence in your ability to handle financial matters.
- **Build an Emergency Fund**: Knowing you have a financial safety net reduces anxiety and builds resilience, allowing you to face unexpected expenses or income fluctuations without panic.

5. **Seeking Support When Needed** Building resilience doesn't mean handling everything alone. Surrounding yourself with supportive people—whether friends, family, or financial advisors—can provide perspective and encouragement, helping you make sound decisions during challenging times.

Chapter 11: Reframing Financial Challenges as Opportunities

Shifting Perspective on Money

In the world of personal finance, challenges are inevitable. Market downturns, unexpected expenses, or even mistakes in judgment are all part of the journey. However, the way we interpret these events can dramatically shape our financial outcomes and overall sense of well-being. By learning to see financial setbacks not as failures but as opportunities for growth, we can foster a mindset that promotes resilience and proactive wealth-building.

Reframing financial challenges involves shifting from a "fixed mindset" that views setbacks as negative, permanent conditions to a "growth mindset" that sees them as temporary, solvable problems. For example, rather than viewing a loss in an investment portfolio as a failure, consider it a valuable lesson in risk tolerance or diversification. Instead of seeing debt as an insurmountable burden, approach it as an opportunity to develop disciplined habits and build financial resilience. With this mindset, each financial experience—good or bad—becomes a stepping stone toward greater financial understanding and mastery.

The positive mindset shift can also reduce the emotional burden of financial stress. Instead of being weighed down by regret or fear, a constructive perspective empowers individuals to focus on the future and take actionable steps toward improvement. When we learn to view financial setbacks as growth opportunities, we become better equipped to make decisions that align with our long-term financial goals.

Techniques for Cognitive Reframing

To embrace this positive perspective, here are practical techniques for cognitive reframing that help transform financial challenges into constructive learning experiences.

1. **Recognize and Label Your Initial Response**
   The first step to reframing is awareness. Recognize and label your immediate emotional response to a financial setback, whether it's fear, frustration, disappointment, or regret. Acknowledging these feelings can help distance yourself from them, allowing for a clearer, more objective perspective.
   - **Example**: If a financial investment hasn't performed as expected, acknowledge your disappointment or frustration. By naming these feelings, you can approach the situation with a sense of curiosity rather than letting emotions dictate your next steps.
2. **Shift the Language You Use Around Money**
   The words we use to describe financial situations impact how we feel and respond. Reframing language helps create a more empowering narrative around financial decisions.
   - **Instead of Saying**: "I failed at budgeting this month," try saying, "I learned where my budgeting needs improvement."
   - **Instead of Thinking**: "I'll never get out of debt," reframe it as, "I'm building habits and making decisions to reduce my debt over time."

- These subtle shifts in language reinforce a growth mindset, making it easier to take constructive action.
3. **Break Down Challenges into Manageable Steps**
   A financial setback can feel overwhelming when viewed as one big issue. By breaking it down into smaller, manageable steps, you can focus on gradual progress rather than feeling paralyzed by the challenge as a whole.
   - **Example**: If you're facing a large debt, break it into smaller, specific repayment goals. Instead of focusing on the total amount, set a goal for the first repayment milestone. This approach helps keep the focus on action, not anxiety.
4. **Practice Perspective-Taking**
   Cognitive reframing involves seeing things from a new perspective. A powerful way to do this is by imagining how someone you respect might view or handle the same situation.
   - **Ask Yourself**: "How would a financially savvy mentor or friend view this situation? What advice might they give me?" This exercise can shift your focus from frustration or regret to proactive problem-solving.
   - Perspective-taking can also include considering your future self. Imagine how you, a year from now, would wish you handled the situation. This longer-term view often encourages more thoughtful responses.
5. **Focus on the Lessons and Growth Opportunities**
   Every financial setback contains a lesson that,

when applied, can improve your financial future. Reflecting on these lessons allows you to shift from self-criticism to self-compassion.
- **Ask Reflective Questions**: "What have I learned from this situation?" or "How can this experience guide my future decisions?" By focusing on learning, you'll turn each setback into a valuable growth experience.
- For instance, if overspending led to credit card debt, use this as a lesson in budgeting or setting up financial safeguards, like automatic transfers to savings.

6. **Practice Visualization to Reinforce a Positive Outcome**

Visualization is a powerful tool for reframing challenges and reinforcing a growth-oriented perspective. When facing a financial obstacle, imagine yourself successfully overcoming it and the positive outcomes that could follow.
- **Visualize Your Goals**: Picture yourself debt-free, financially secure, or confidently investing with knowledge. This positive visualization not only reduces immediate stress but also helps remind you of your motivation for pursuing financial goals.
- **See Setbacks as Stepping Stones**: Imagine each setback as a staircase leading to your goals, with each step providing greater insight and resilience.

7. **Celebrate Small Wins Along the Way**

Reframing doesn't mean ignoring progress. Even small successes should be acknowledged and celebrated as part of your overall financial journey. Small wins help reinforce a sense of

accomplishment and provide motivation during challenging periods.
- **Track Progress**: Keep a log of milestones, whether it's saving a certain amount, paying down part of a debt, or resisting an impulse purchase. Celebrate these achievements, however small, as evidence of your growth and resilience.
- **Reward Yourself**: Acknowledge and reward your progress. Positive reinforcement can build confidence and help sustain momentum as you work toward long-term goals.

Chapter 12: Strengthening Emotional Intelligence in Financial Choices

The Power of EQ in Money Management
Emotional intelligence (EQ) is the ability to recognize, understand, and manage our emotions and those of others, and it plays a central role in making rational and effective financial decisions. High EQ enables us to make choices aligned with long-term goals, even in the face of emotional triggers like fear, greed, or impatience. In the financial context, EQ involves three key skills: self-awareness, self-regulation, and empathy.

1. **Self-Awareness**
   Self-awareness is the foundation of emotional intelligence. It allows individuals to understand their emotions and recognize how these feelings influence financial behaviors. For instance, a self-aware person may notice that they're prone to impulsive spending when stressed or that they become overly conservative with investments during market volatility. This awareness acts as a "pause button," giving space to evaluate whether an emotional reaction is helpful or counterproductive.

2. **Self-Regulation**
   Self-regulation is the ability to manage one's emotions in a constructive way. It involves resisting impulsive reactions and maintaining focus on long-term financial goals. For example, rather than making a quick decision to sell stocks in a panic, a self-regulated individual would wait until the emotional reaction subsides, allowing for a more rational, deliberate choice. Self-regulation also

helps prevent reactive spending or risky investments made out of fear or FOMO (fear of missing out).

3. **Empathy**
   Empathy—understanding others' emotions—is less often associated with financial choices but is crucial for sound financial relationships and decision-making. Empathy allows people to consider the perspectives of family members, partners, or business associates when making joint financial decisions, fostering collaboration and mutual understanding. In situations like estate planning, family budgeting, or financial caregiving, empathy helps individuals balance their own goals with the needs of others, leading to more harmonious outcomes.

By cultivating these EQ skills, individuals can make financial decisions that are less reactive and more aligned with their values and goals. A high EQ enables people to manage their emotions and respond thoughtfully, leading to greater financial stability, resilience, and satisfaction.

Building EQ in Financial Life

Here are some exercises and practices that help build emotional intelligence, focusing on self-awareness, self-regulation, and empathy. Strengthening EQ takes time, but these techniques make it easier to approach financial decisions with clarity, calm, and compassion.

1. **Practice Financial Self-Reflection**
   Reflective practices are essential for building self-awareness in financial decisions. Regular self-

reflection can help individuals recognize patterns in their behavior, understand triggers, and learn from past experiences.

- **Set Up a Reflection Routine**: At the end of each month, take some time to review major financial decisions, asking questions like, "What emotions did I feel before, during, and after this decision?" and "Did my choices align with my long-term goals?"
- **Create a Financial Reflection Journal**: Keep a dedicated journal to record these reflections. This helps track patterns over time, making it easier to see where emotional triggers arise and which areas of money management require more attention.
- **Evaluate Past Decisions Without Judgment**: When reflecting, focus on observing patterns rather than criticizing yourself. This mindset fosters self-awareness without self-blame, making it easier to make adjustments moving forward.

2. **Set Personal Guidelines for Financial Self-Regulation**

Developing self-regulation in financial matters means creating habits and guidelines that help you avoid emotional reactions and impulsive decisions.

- **Establish a "Cooling-Off" Period for Major Purchases**: Implement a rule that requires a 24-hour waiting period before making any non-essential purchase over a certain amount. This practice helps ensure that spending aligns with financial goals, giving time for emotions like excitement or anxiety to subside.

- **Define Your Financial "Non-Negotiables"**: Identify the spending, saving, or investing principles that support your goals, like maintaining an emergency fund or limiting entertainment expenses. When emotions arise, these principles act as guardrails, helping you make grounded, values-based choices.
- **Visualize Consequences and Benefits**: Before making a decision, visualize both the potential benefits and downsides. For example, imagine the regret that might follow an impulsive purchase or the satisfaction of a well-planned investment. Visualization helps slow down impulsive tendencies and encourages mindful decision-making.

3. **Use Empathy to Improve Financial Relationships**

Empathy strengthens relationships and aids in making collaborative financial decisions, which is particularly important in family budgeting or joint investment planning.

- **Perspective-Taking in Joint Financial Decisions**: When making decisions with others, like a partner or family member, actively try to understand their perspective. For example, if your partner is hesitant about a major purchase, consider their concerns rather than reacting defensively. Perspective-taking can foster understanding and lead to compromises that respect both parties' values.

- **Hold Monthly Financial "Check-ins" with Loved Ones**: Set up regular meetings to review financial plans, budgets, or goals with any financial partners. These check-ins allow both parties to discuss goals and concerns openly, preventing misunderstandings and promoting empathy.
- **Practice Active Listening**: During financial discussions, practice fully listening to others before responding. This helps ensure that everyone feels heard, improving trust and collaboration, especially in situations that may involve differing viewpoints or goals.

4. **Work with "What-If" Scenarios for Emotional Preparedness**

This exercise builds both self-regulation and empathy by helping you mentally prepare for potential financial setbacks or opportunities.

- **Imagine Potential Outcomes**: For example, consider how you would feel if your investments dropped in value. By rehearsing this scenario in your mind, you can prepare for emotional reactions and practice self-regulation. Ask yourself, "How will I react, and what strategies can I use to stay calm?"
- **Practice Reassuring Language**: Imagine discussing these scenarios with a friend or loved one, using supportive language. Phrasing like "Even if the market fluctuates, we're on track for the long term" helps reinforce a balanced perspective that combines empathy with clear-headedness.

5. **Strengthen Self-Awareness with Daily Emotional Check-Ins**

Emotionomics :How Feelings Drive Financial Choices

Regularly checking in with your emotions helps you build self-awareness, a cornerstone of EQ, by revealing any underlying feelings that may affect your financial decisions.

- **Set Aside a Few Minutes Each Day**: At the beginning or end of each day, take a few moments to note how you're feeling. Are you anxious, optimistic, or frustrated? Identifying these emotions creates awareness, making it less likely that you'll make impulsive decisions based on these feelings.
- **Ask Yourself Reflective Questions**: When you're aware of specific feelings—like stress over an upcoming expense—ask yourself questions like, "What's causing this feeling? Is there a constructive way to address it?" This practice brings attention to the emotions at play and helps create a clear separation between feeling and acting.

6. **Celebrate and Learn from Financial Wins and Losses**

   Reviewing both positive and negative financial outcomes with a growth mindset reinforces all three EQ skills—self-awareness, self-regulation, and empathy.

   - **Acknowledge Emotional Wins**: Did you resist the urge to splurge or stick to your savings plan during a difficult month? Celebrating these small wins builds self-awareness and reinforces the value of self-regulation.
   - **Reframe Financial Losses**: Instead of viewing losses or mistakes as failures, see them as learning experiences. This shift

promotes self-compassion, helping you manage emotions constructively and avoid self-doubt.
- **Practice Empathy Toward Yourself**: Be kind to yourself when evaluating financial decisions, especially during challenging times. Just as empathy toward others strengthens relationships, self-empathy encourages confidence, resilience, and healthier financial habits.

Part 4: Building a Balanced, Fulfilling Relationship with Money

Chapter 13: Rethinking Wealth Beyond Monetary Success

Redefining What it Means to Be Wealthy
In today's world, wealth is often seen as the accumulation of money and possessions. Yet, this narrow view of wealth overlooks many aspects of a balanced, fulfilling life. True wealth encompasses more than financial assets—it includes a sense of security, emotional well-being, meaningful relationships, and a lifestyle that aligns with one's values. Shifting the perspective on wealth to embrace these elements can lead to a more rewarding, resilient approach to money.

Wealth can provide freedom and security, but its value is diminished if it comes at the expense of health, peace of mind, or relationships. When people define wealth solely in monetary terms, they may experience chronic stress, sacrifice personal happiness, or strain relationships in the pursuit of more. Financial well-being should support life satisfaction, not overshadow it. By broadening the definition of wealth to include balance and fulfillment, individuals can pursue financial goals without losing sight of what truly matters.

Encouraging readers to adopt this more holistic view of wealth can help them redefine success as the ability to enjoy a life that is balanced, meaningful, and secure. This shift can ease the pressures that stem from comparing financial status or possessions with others and create a deeper sense of satisfaction and peace.

Finding Personal Meaning in Financial Success

To achieve a balanced and meaningful relationship with wealth, it's essential for readers to define success on their own terms, looking beyond materialistic benchmarks. This involves understanding what truly brings fulfillment, whether it's health, strong relationships, personal growth, or contributing to a cause. Here are ways to encourage readers to find personal meaning in their financial journey:

1. **Reflect on Personal Values and Aspirations**
   Financial goals should align with individual values and aspirations, creating a sense of purpose beyond wealth accumulation. Encourage readers to reflect on questions such as:
   - "What does a fulfilling life look like to me?"
   - "Which aspects of life bring me the most happiness and contentment?"
   - "How does financial stability contribute to, or detract from, my well-being?" These reflections help clarify what financial success truly means on a personal level and establish goals that honor these values.

2. **Prioritize Security and Peace of Mind Over Excess**
   For many, peace of mind is one of the most valuable aspects of financial security. Rather than striving for excessive wealth, readers can focus on establishing financial habits that bring long-term stability and security. This might mean:
   - Building an emergency fund that provides confidence during unexpected setbacks.
   - Avoiding unnecessary financial risks that lead to stress or uncertainty.

- Practicing financial habits that support peace of mind, such as spending within a budget, investing steadily, and reducing debt.

3. **Consider Health as a Core Aspect of Wealth**
   Health is often overlooked as part of wealth, but without it, financial success loses much of its value. Encouraging readers to invest in their physical and mental well-being aligns with a balanced approach to wealth. Health-related goals might include:
   - Allocating funds for regular healthcare and wellness activities, such as gym memberships, nutritious foods, and preventive checkups.
   - Recognizing that financial stress can impact health and seeking ways to reduce it by simplifying finances, setting realistic goals, and cultivating healthy financial habits.
   - Viewing health as a form of wealth, which increases life satisfaction and longevity, supporting long-term financial stability.

4. **Value Relationships as a Key Component of Wealth**
   Meaningful relationships contribute to a rich and fulfilling life and should be prioritized alongside financial goals. Healthy relationships provide support, purpose, and joy, all of which contribute to a sense of abundance that money alone can't achieve. To integrate relationships into one's definition of wealth, consider:
   - Prioritizing time with family and friends over the pursuit of excessive work hours or financial ambition.

- Cultivating generosity by using wealth to support loved ones, whether through shared experiences or assistance during times of need.
- Emphasizing the value of strong personal connections over material comparisons, such as by focusing on shared values instead of lifestyle competition.

5. **Embrace Experiences and Growth Over Material Accumulation**

    Research shows that experiences, rather than material possessions, tend to bring more lasting happiness and fulfillment. By placing value on personal growth and meaningful experiences, individuals can achieve a sense of wealth that enriches life on a deeper level.
    - Encourage readers to invest in experiences that align with their values, whether it's travel, education, hobbies, or charitable endeavors.
    - Suggest creating memories and learning opportunities as ways to feel enriched without focusing solely on material wealth.
    - Remind readers that true wealth is an ongoing journey, marked by experiences that contribute to lifelong growth and fulfillment rather than fleeting status symbols.

6. **Cultivate Inner Peace and Contentment as Part of Financial Success**

    Inner peace and contentment are essential to a balanced sense of wealth, helping to alleviate financial anxiety and reduce the pressures of comparison. When individuals cultivate a sense of satisfaction with what they have, they feel a greater sense of abundance.

- Practice gratitude for current financial security, health, relationships, and achievements. A gratitude journal can be a helpful tool to keep focused on what already enriches life.
- Set goals that focus on quality of life rather than quantity, fostering contentment with progress and growth instead of unattainable perfection.
- Encourage readers to avoid the trap of "moving goalposts," which is the constant pursuit of the next financial milestone without appreciating existing achievements. By celebrating milestones as they come, readers can maintain a balanced outlook on success.

Chapter 14: Practicing Gratitude and Contentment in Financial Life

The Value of Appreciation and Contentment
Gratitude and contentment are powerful antidotes to the feelings of greed, envy, and dissatisfaction that often arise in our financial lives. When we focus on what we already have, we naturally become less fixated on acquiring more, which can lead to wiser financial choices and greater peace of mind. Practicing gratitude helps shift focus from what we lack to what we have achieved, both financially and personally, allowing us to recognize the abundance in our lives.

Gratitude is a tool for combating materialistic pressures and the constant "more is better" mentality that drives overspending and unnecessary financial risks. When we cultivate appreciation for our current financial state, we are less likely to compare ourselves with others or feel inadequate based on someone else's success. This shift can reduce impulse purchases, debt, and financial stress.

Contentment, on the other hand, fosters satisfaction with what we have, leading to a more stable financial approach. It encourages us to set realistic financial goals and make decisions aligned with personal values, not societal expectations. By practicing gratitude and contentment, readers can build a financial mindset that emphasizes sustainability and satisfaction rather than endless accumulation.

Daily Practices to Foster Financial Peace

Here are some simple, effective daily practices for cultivating gratitude and contentment in financial life. These routines help shift focus to non-material achievements, values, and the aspects of wealth that truly bring fulfillment.

1. **Start a Gratitude Journal**

   A gratitude journal is a powerful tool for fostering appreciation and contentment in your daily life. By dedicating just a few minutes each day to jot down what you're grateful for, you can begin to see your financial life from a more balanced and positive perspective.

   - **How to Begin**: Each day, write down three things you're grateful for. These don't have to be directly related to finances but could include elements of financial stability, like a job that meets your needs, a comfortable home, or the freedom to enjoy small luxuries. Over time, this habit builds awareness of the positive aspects of your financial life.
   - **Shift Focus to Non-Material Wealth**: Include items in your journal that aren't related to money or possessions, such as supportive relationships, good health, or personal growth. This practice reminds you of the richness in life beyond financial measures.

2. **Practice Mindful Spending**

   Mindful spending is the practice of consciously considering each purchase, which encourages both gratitude and contentment. Before making a purchase, take a moment to reflect on its necessity and alignment with your values.

- **Pause Before Spending**: If you feel an urge to buy something, pause and consider why. Ask yourself, "Am I buying this to fill an emotional void, or does it truly align with my needs and values?" This reflection helps avoid impulsive purchases driven by envy, boredom, or societal pressure.
- **Reflect on Past Purchases**: At the end of each week, reflect on a purchase that brought genuine value to your life. This reflection encourages appreciation for thoughtful spending and reinforces a habit of making intentional financial choices.

3. **Create a "Sufficiency List"**

   A sufficiency list is a record of things you currently have that fulfill your needs and wants, fostering a sense of contentment with your current financial state.

   - **How to Make a Sufficiency List**: Write down areas of your life where you feel contentment. For example, you might list your home, transportation, health, or supportive friends and family. This list acts as a reminder of the abundance you already have and reduces the urge to constantly pursue more.
   - **Revisit Your List Regularly**: Review your list periodically to reinforce a sense of sufficiency and contentment. Adding new items when you feel satisfied with aspects of your life can deepen your appreciation.

4. **Engage in Small Acts of Generosity**

   Practicing generosity is a direct way to experience gratitude for your financial stability while shifting focus away from accumulation. Giving to others, whether in the form of time, resources, or money, cultivates feelings of abundance and fulfillment.

- **Ways to Give**: You don't have to give large amounts to feel the impact of generosity. Small acts like buying coffee for a friend, donating to a cause you care about, or volunteering can foster a greater sense of purpose and satisfaction with your own financial situation.
- **Reflect on the Experience**: After giving, take a moment to reflect on how it felt and how it contributed to your own sense of fulfillment. Generosity reminds us that wealth is not solely about accumulation but also about the ability to share and support others.

5. **Celebrate Financial Milestones—Big and Small**
Celebrating financial achievements, no matter how modest, builds gratitude for progress and reinforces a sense of financial contentment. This practice keeps you focused on the journey rather than constantly seeking the next big goal.

- **Recognize Progress Regularly**: Whether it's paying off a small debt, increasing your savings by a certain percentage, or simply sticking to your budget, take time to acknowledge these successes. Celebrating these wins helps you appreciate the journey, reinforcing contentment with your progress.
- **Set Up Meaningful Rewards**: Mark each milestone with a small reward that aligns with your values, such as a favorite treat, a day out, or simply time spent doing

something you enjoy. These rewards make the journey toward financial goals more fulfilling and sustainable.

6. **Practice Contentment Affirmations**
Daily affirmations are a powerful way to reframe your perspective on wealth and reinforce contentment. These affirmations can serve as reminders to appreciate what you already have.
    - **Examples of Affirmations**: "I am grateful for the financial security I currently have," or "I have enough to meet my needs, and I am content with what I have." These positive statements counterbalance feelings of lack, helping to develop a healthier, more appreciative financial mindset.
    - **Incorporate Affirmations into Your Routine**: Repeat affirmations each morning or evening as part of a routine. Consistency helps reinforce contentment and gratitude, grounding you in a mindset of "enough" rather than "more."

7. **Shift Focus from Possessions to Experiences**
Research shows that experiences often bring more lasting satisfaction than material possessions. Investing in experiences that align with your values can increase contentment and reduce the need for physical accumulation.
    - **Prioritize Experience Over Acquisition**: Spend on experiences that provide lasting memories and align with your values, like trips, learning opportunities, or meaningful activities with loved ones.
    - **Reflect on Positive Memories**: Regularly revisit past experiences you're grateful for,

whether through journaling or simply taking a moment to recall a fond memory. This practice reinforces the idea that wealth is not about material items but about moments and memories that enrich life.

Chapter 15: Making Intentional Financial Choices Through Mindfulness

The Impact of Mindful Money Management
In a world filled with constant financial temptations, pressures, and choices, practicing mindfulness can transform how we handle money. Mindfulness is the practice of staying fully present and aware of our thoughts, emotions, and surroundings, and applying this approach to finances means making choices that are deliberate and aligned with our values. Instead of reacting impulsively to financial triggers—like sales, social pressures, or stress—mindful money management encourages us to consider each decision carefully, fostering a healthier and more intentional approach to spending, saving, and investing.

When we practice mindfulness with our finances, we're more likely to make values-driven choices. For example, mindful spending may mean allocating resources toward experiences or items that bring lasting fulfillment rather than temporary satisfaction. Mindful saving means setting aside money in ways that genuinely support our future goals, rather than hoarding or saving out of fear. Mindful investing involves aligning investment decisions with our financial objectives and risk tolerance rather than making choices based on market hype or fear of missing out. This thoughtful approach helps reduce financial stress, improves long-term financial well-being, and fosters a more fulfilling relationship with money.

Mindful money management also brings clarity, helping us prioritize financial actions that support our core values. This intentionality can prevent the regret that often follows impulsive financial decisions and create a sense of peace, satisfaction, and purpose in our financial lives.

Practical Steps for Financial Mindfulness

Here are some simple yet powerful practices for bringing mindfulness to everyday financial choices, helping you make thoughtful, intentional decisions that align with your values and long-term goals.

1. **Pause Before Purchases**
   One of the most effective mindfulness techniques is to pause before making a purchase, especially for non-essential items. This pause creates space to assess the motivation behind your spending.
   - **Practice the "24-Hour Rule"**: For any non-essential purchase, wait at least 24 hours before buying. This delay helps curb impulsive spending and allows time to evaluate if the purchase aligns with your goals or if it's driven by temporary emotions.
   - **Ask Intentional Questions**: During the pause, ask yourself questions like, "Do I truly need this item?" or "Does this purchase support my values or financial goals?" These questions help bring awareness to the decision-making process, making it easier to avoid impulsive buys.
2. **Set Financial Intentions Aligned with Your Values**
   Setting intentions is a cornerstone of mindful money management. By defining what matters most to you financially, you can make choices that reflect these

priorities, enhancing satisfaction and reducing regret.

- **Identify Core Financial Values**: Consider what financial success means to you beyond just accumulating money. It could include security, freedom, family support, or charitable giving. By identifying these core values, you create a framework for intentional financial choices.
- **Write Down Your Financial Intentions**: Document specific intentions related to these values, such as "I want to save to provide security for my family" or "I will avoid purchases that don't align with my minimalist lifestyle." Reviewing these intentions regularly reinforces mindful decision-making.

3. **Establish Regular Financial Check-Ins** Mindfulness requires ongoing reflection. By setting aside time each week or month to review your financial habits, you can assess whether your choices align with your goals and adjust as needed.

- **Conduct Monthly Financial Reviews**: Each month, take time to review your spending, saving, and investment behaviors. Reflect on whether your choices align with your intentions and identify any adjustments needed.
- **Ask Reflective Questions**: During these check-ins, consider questions like, "Am I happy with how I used my money this month?" or "Did my financial choices reflect my long-term goals?" This exercise creates awareness of habits and helps build a pattern of intentional financial behavior.

4. **Track Emotional Spending Patterns**
Many financial choices are driven by emotions like stress, boredom, or excitement, leading to impulsive purchases or unnecessary expenses. By identifying these triggers, you can better manage emotional spending.
    - **Keep a Spending Journal**: Track non-essential purchases and note the emotions you felt before, during, and after each one. Were you feeling stressed, excited, or bored? This journal can reveal emotional patterns, helping you identify where to introduce mindfulness.
    - **Use Emotion-Based Decision-Making Techniques**: For example, if you notice a pattern of spending when you're bored, plan activities that don't involve spending to manage that trigger. This awareness reduces emotional spending and promotes mindful financial choices.
5. **Align Spending with Financial Goals**
Mindful money management involves evaluating purchases in the context of long-term goals, such as saving for retirement, paying off debt, or building an emergency fund. By aligning spending with these goals, you create a more purpose-driven approach to finances.
    - **Create a Financial Vision Board**: Visual representations of your financial goals (like images of a debt-free lifestyle, a dream home, or travel plans) can help you stay focused on what you're working toward. Each time you're tempted to spend impulsively, take a moment to reflect on this

vision board and remind yourself of your priorities.
- **Implement "Goal-Based Spending"**: Before making a purchase, ask, "How does this support my financial goals?" If it doesn't align, consider postponing or eliminating it. This technique keeps spending focused on what truly matters, making financial choices more intentional.

6. **Practice Gratitude for Financial Security**
Practicing gratitude for your current financial situation, no matter its stage, reinforces a mindful approach to finances. When you appreciate what you have, you're less likely to feel pressure to acquire more.
    - **Start a Financial Gratitude Journal**: Each day or week, write down one aspect of your financial life that you're grateful for, such as your job, a savings account, or a supportive family. This practice encourages mindfulness, reducing the need for constant accumulation.
    - **Shift to a "Sufficiency Mindset"**: Instead of focusing on what you lack, remind yourself of what you already have. This mindset shift can reduce impulse spending and help you make choices that support long-term stability over short-term desires.

7. **Meditate on Financial Goals and Decisions**
Mindfulness meditation can also be applied to financial goals and decision-making. Spending a few minutes visualizing your goals or calming your mind before a major financial decision helps you make choices that are thoughtful and grounded.

- **Set Aside Time for Financial Visualization**: Visualize yourself achieving your financial goals, such as becoming debt-free, building savings, or investing wisely. This exercise reinforces your commitment to these goals and creates a stronger connection between your daily choices and long-term vision.
- **Use Mindfulness Techniques Before Major Decisions**: Before making a big purchase or investment, close your eyes, take a few deep breaths, and let your mind settle. This practice helps clear emotions and supports a more rational, values-driven choice.

Conclusion: The Path to Emotional Mastery in Financial Decisions

Embracing Emotional Mastery for Financial Well-being
Achieving financial well-being requires more than just smart budgeting or strategic investments—it demands emotional mastery. Throughout this journey, we've explored how emotions like fear, greed, envy, and impulsiveness can influence financial choices, often leading to stress, regret, or instability. By understanding and managing these emotions, we can make more intentional, values-aligned decisions that support long-term security and fulfillment.

Emotional mastery in finance is about recognizing that wealth isn't just a number; it's a balanced state of mind and lifestyle. By developing self-awareness, self-regulation, and empathy, we gain control over the emotional triggers that can otherwise lead to hasty or unwise decisions. A mindset rooted in emotional mastery transforms our relationship with money, encouraging us to view it as a tool to support a meaningful, fulfilling life rather than a source of anxiety or competition. This balanced, emotionally aware approach allows us to navigate financial highs and lows with resilience, ensuring that our choices are grounded in both rational thought and inner peace.

Commitment to Lifelong Financial Emotional Awareness
Emotional mastery is a continuous journey, one that requires dedication to lifelong learning and self-reflection. As our financial circumstances and goals evolve, so too will

the emotions we experience around money. Cultivating a lasting practice of emotional awareness, self-discipline, and mindfulness empowers us to adapt with wisdom, preventing temporary feelings from overshadowing our long-term vision.

Encouraging readers to embrace this commitment means reminding them that financial freedom is ultimately about having control over both their resources and their reactions. True wealth is grounded in an emotionally aware approach that emphasizes gratitude, purpose, and security over accumulation for its own sake. Through mindfulness practices, regular self-reflection, and ongoing learning, we can continue to grow not just in financial stability but also in self-understanding and resilience.

By nurturing emotional awareness, we empower ourselves to make intentional choices that reflect our deepest values and priorities, leading to a sense of financial freedom that is not just measured in dollars but in peace of mind and life satisfaction. In the end, mastering the emotions that drive our financial decisions unlocks a wealth of fulfillment, purpose, and stability—an abundant, balanced relationship with money that enriches every aspect of our lives.

www.ingramcontent.com/pod-product-compliance
Lightning Source LLC
Chambersburg PA
CBHW070422240526
45472CB00020B/1149